GLAD OF THESE TIMES

Helen Dunmore is a poet, novelist and children's writer. Her poetry books have been given the Poetry Book Society Choice and Recommendations, Cardiff International Poetry Prize, Alice Hunt Bartlett Award and Signal Poetry Award, and *Bestiary* was shortlisted for the T.S. Eliot Prize. Her latest Bloodaxe poetry titles are *Out of the Blue: Poems 1975-2001* (2001) and *Glad of These Times* (2007).

She has published nine novels and three books of short stories with Viking Penguin, including *Zennor in Darkness* (1993), *A Spell of Winter* (1995), *Talking to the Dead* (1996), *The Siege* (2001), *Mourning Ruby* (2003) and *House of Orphans* (2006). She won the McKitterick Prize for *Zennor in Darkness* and the Orange Prize for *A Spell of Winter*.

HELEN DUNMORE

GLAD OF THESE TIMES

BLOODAXE BOOKS

ISBN: 978 1 85224 758 4

First published 2007 by
Bloodaxe Books Ltd,
Highgreen,
Tarset,
Northumberland NE48 1RP.

Second impression 2007

www.bloodaxebooks.com
For further information about Bloodaxe titles
please visit our website or write to
the above address for a catalogue.

Bloodaxe Books Ltd acknowledges
the financial assistance of
Arts Council England, North East.

Cover design: Neil Astley & Pamela Robertson-Pearce.

Cover printing: J. Thomson Colour Printers Ltd, Glasgow.

Printed in Great Britain by
Bell & Bain Limited, Glasgow, Scotland.

For Maurice Dunmore

1928-2006

ACKNOWLEDGEMENTS

Acknowledgements are due to the editors of the following publications, in which some of these poems first appeared: *Being Alive: the sequel to 'Staying Alive'* (Bloodaxe Books, 2004), *City: Bristol Today in Poems and Pictures* (Paralalia, 2004), *La Traductière, Light Unlocked: Christmas Card Poems* (Enitharmon Press, 2005), *The Long Field* (Great Atlantic Publications), *New Delta Review*, *Poetry* (Chicago), *Poetry Review* and *The Way You Say the World: A Celebration for Anne Stevenson* (Shoestring Press, 2003).

CONTENTS

City lilacs

In crack-haunted alleys, overhangs,
plots of sour earth that pass for gardens,
in the space between wall and wheelie bin,

where men with mobiles make urgent conversation,
where bare-legged girls shiver in April winds,
where a new mother stands on her doorstep and blinks
at the brightness of morning, so suddenly born –

in all these places the city lilacs are pushing
their cones of blossom into the spring
to be taken by the warm wind.

Lilac, like love, makes no distinction.
It will open for anyone.
Even before love knows that it is love
lilac knows it must blossom.

In crack-haunted alleys, in overhangs,
in somebody's front garden
abandoned to crisp packets and cans,

on landscaped motorway roundabouts,
in the depth of parks
where men and women are lost in transactions
of flesh and cash, where mobiles ring

and the deal is done – here the city lilacs
release their sweet, wild perfume
then bow down, heavy with rain.

Crossing the field

To live your life is not as simple as to cross a field.
RUSSIAN PROVERB

To cross the field on a sunset of spider-webs
sprung and shining, thistle heads
white with tufts that are harvest
tended and brought to fruit by no one,

to cross the long field as the sun goes down
and the whale-back Scillies show damson
twenty miles off, as the wind sculls
out back, and five lighthouses
one by one open their eyes,

to cross the long field as it darkens
when rooks are homeward, and gulls
swing out from the tilt of land
to the breast of ocean – now is the time
the vixen stirs, and the green lane's
vivid with footprints.

A field is enough to spend a life in.
Harrow, granite and mattress springs,
shards and bones, turquoise droppings
from pigeons that gorge on nightshade berries,
a charm of goldfinch, a flight of linnets,
fieldfare and January redwing
venturing westward in the dusk,
all are folded in the dark of the field,

all are folded into the dark of the field
and need more days
to paint them, than life gives.

Litany

For the length of time it takes a bruise to fade
for the heavy weight on getting out of bed,
for the hair's grey, for the skin's tired grain,
for the spider naevus and drinker's nose
for the vocabulary of palliation and Macmillan
for friends who know the best funeral readings,

for the everydayness of pain, for waiting patiently
to ask the pharmacist about your medication
for elastic bandages and ulcer dressings,
for knowing what to say
when your friend says how much she still misses him,
for needing a coat although it is warm,

for the length of time it takes a wound to heal,
for the strange pity you feel
when told off by the blank sure faces
of the young who own and know everything,
for the bare flesh of the next generation,
for the word 'generation', which used to mean nothing.

Don't count John among the dreams

(i.m. John Kipling, son of Rudyard Kipling,
who died in the Battle of Loos in 1915)

Don't count John among the dreams
a parent cherishes for his children –
that they will be different from him,
not poets but the stuff of poems.

Don't count John among the dreams
of leaders, warriors, eagle-eyed stalkers
picking up the track of lions.
Even in the zoo he can barely see them –

his eyes, like yours, are half-blind.
Short, obedient, hirsute
how he would love to delight you.
He reads every word you write.

Don't count John among your dreams.
Don't wangle a commission for him,
don't wangle a death for him.
He is barely eighteen.

Without his spectacles, after a shell-blast,
he will be seen one more time
before the next shell sees to him.
Wounding, weeping from pain,

he will be able to see nothing.
And you will always mourn him.
You will write a poem.
You will count him into your dreams.

The other side of the sky's dark room

On the other side of the sky's dark room
a monstrous finger
of lightning plays war.

As clay quivers
beaded with moisture
where the spade slices it

the night quivers.
Late, towards midnight, a door slams
on the other side of the sky's dark room.

The spade stretchers
raw earth, helpless to ease
the dark, inward explosion.

Convolvulus

I love these flowers that lie in the dust.
We think the world is what we wish it is,
we think that where we say flowers, there will be flowers,
where we say bombs, there will be nothing
until we turn to reconstruction.
But here on the ground, in the dust
is the striped, lilac convolvulus.

Believe me, how fragrant it is,
the flower of coming up from the beach.
There in the dust the convolvulus squeezes itself shut.
You go by, you see nothing, you are tired
from that last swim too late in the evening.

Where we say bombs, there will be bombs.
The only decision is where to plant them –
these flowers that grow at the whim of our fingers –
but not the roving thread of the convolvulus,
spun from a source we cannot trace.

Below, at the foot of the cliff
the sea laps up the apron of sand
which was our day's home. Where we said land
water has come, where we said flower
and snapped our fingers, there came nothing.

I love these flowers that lie in the dust
barefaced at noon, candid convolvulus
lilac and striped and flattened underfoot.
Crushed, they breathe out their honey, and slowly
come back to themselves in the balm of the night.
But a lumber of engines grows in the seaward sky –
how huge the engines, huge the shadow of planes.

The grey lilo

The grey lilo with scarlet and violet
paintballed into its hollows, on which
my daughter floats, from which her delicate wrist
angles, while her hand sculls the water,

the grey lilo where my daughter floats,
her wet hair smooth to her skull,
her eyes closed, their dark lashes
protecting her from the sky's envy
of their sudden, staggering blue,

the grey lilo, misted with condensation,
idly shadows the floor of the pool
as if it had a journey to go on –
but no, it is only catching the echo
of scarlet and violet geraniums,

and my daughter is only singing
under her breath, and the time that settles
like yellow butterflies, is only
just about to move on –

Yellow butterflies

They are the sun's fingerprints on grey pebbles
two yards from the water,
dabbed on the eucalyptus, the olive,
the cracked pot of marigolds,
and now they pulse again, sucking
dry the wild thyme,

or on a sightless bird, not yet buried
they feast a while.

If they have a name, these yellow butterflies,
they do not want it; they know what they are,
quivering, sated, and now once more
printing sun, sun, and again sun
in the olive hollows.

Plume

If you were to reach up your hand,
if you were to push apart the leaves
turning aside your face like one who looks
not at the sun but where the sun hides –
there, where the spider scuttles
and the lizard whips out of sight –

if you were to search
with your small, brown, inexperienced hands
among the leaves that shield the fire of the fruit
in a vault of shadow, if you were to do it
you'd be allowed, for this is your planet
and you are new on it,

if you were to reach inside the leaves
and cup your hands as the fruit descends
like a balloon on the fields of evening
huffing its orange plume
one last time, as the flight ends
and the fruit stops growing –

Odysseus

For those who do not write poems
but have the cause of poems in them:
this thief, sly as Odysseus
who puts out from Albanian waters
into the grape-dark Ionian dawn,
his dirty engine coughing out puffs of black,
to maraud, as his ancestors taught him,
the soft villas of the south —

The blue garden

'Doesn't it look peaceful?' someone said
as our train halted on the embankment
and there was nothing to do but stare
at the blue garden.

Blue roses slowly opened,
blue apples glistened
beneath the spreading peacock of leaves.

The fountain spat jets of pure Prussian
the decking was made with fingers of midnight
the grass was as blue as Kentucky.

Even the children playing
in their ultramarine paddling-pool
were touched by a cobalt Midas

who had changed their skin
from the warm colours of earth
to the azure of heaven.

'Don't they look happy?' someone said,
as the train manager apologised
for the inconvenience caused to our journey,

and yes, they looked happy.
Didn't we wish we were in the blue garden
soaked in the spray of the hose-snake,

didn't we wish we could dig in the indigo earth
for sky-coloured potatoes,
didn't we wish our journey was over

and we were free to race down the embankment
and be caught up in the blue, like those children
who shrank to dots of cerulean
as our train got going.

Violets

Sometimes, but rarely, the ancestors
who set my bones, and that kink
where my parting won't stay straight – strangers
whose blood beats like mine –
call out for flowers
after the work of a lifetime.

Many lifetimes, and I don't know them –
the pubs they kept, the market stalls they abandoned,
the cattle driven and service taken,
the mines and rumours and disappearances
of men gone looking for work.

If they left papers, these have dissolved.
Maybe on census nights they were walking
from town to town, on their way elsewhere.
Where they left their bones, who knows.

I can call them up, but they won't answer.
They want the touch of other hands, that rubbed
their quick harsh lives to brightness.
They have no interest in being ancestors.
They have given enough.

But this I know about: a bunch of violets
laid on a grave, and a woman walking,
and black rain falling on the headstone
of 'the handsomest man I've ever seen'.

The rowan

(in memory of Michael Donaghy)

The rowan, weary of blossoming
is thick with berries now, in bronze September
where the sky has been left to harden,
hammered, ground down
to fine metal, blue-tanned.

In the nakedness beneath the rowan
grow pale cyclamen
and autumn crocus, bare-stemmed.
Beaten, fragile, the flowers still come
eager for blossoming.

Weary of blossoming, the rowan
holds its blood-red tattoo of berries.
No evil can cross this threshold.
The rowan, the lovely rowan
will bring protection.

Barnoon

We are the grown-ups, they the children
sent to bed while the sun is shining,
with a quilt to keep them warm.

We are the clothed, and they the naked.
Their dress of flesh has slipped off.
If they had a shroud, it has rotted.

We are old beside the purity of their hope,
those drowned mariners
anchored in salvation,

we bring nothing but a stare
of fickle, transient wonder,
but they make their own flowers –

a flush of primroses,
dog violets, foxgloves
taller than children, rusty montbretia –

and at Christmas they give birth
to the first daffodils
startled from the earth.

Getting into the car

No, they won't gather their white skirts
before stooping to enter
the deep-buttoned wedding car,

having placed their flowers
in the bridesmaid's fingers,
hand-tied, unravelling.

They won't wipe the delicate sweat
of condensation, and wave
one last time,

no, not for them the fat-tyred Mercedes
or mothers swooping to bless
with tweaks and kisses.

How the wedding car smells of skin
and heat, and dry-cleaning of suits –
but no, it will not happen.

Girls, it is your fortune
to be outside a club at 3 A.M.
to be spangled and beautiful

but to pick the wrong men,
to get into the car with them
and go where they are going

over the black river, under the black river
where your eyes will be wiped of sight
and your bodies of breathing.

Glad of these times

Driving along the motorway
swerving the packed lanes
I am glad of these times.

Because I did not die in childbirth
because my children will survive me
I am glad of these times.

I am not hungry, I do not curtsey,
I lock my door with my own key
and I am glad of these times,

glad of central heating and cable TV
glad of e-mail and keyhole surgery
glad of power showers and washing machines,

glad of polio inoculations
glad of three weeks' paid holiday
glad of smart cards and cashback,

glad of twenty types of yoghurt
glad of cheap flights to Prague
glad that I work.

I do not breathe pure air or walk green lanes,
see darkness, hear silence,
make music, tell stories,

tend the dead in their dying
tend the newborn in their birthing,
tend the fire in its breathing,

but I am glad of my times,
these times, the age
we feel in our bones, our rage

of tyre music, speed
annulling the peasant graves
of all my ancestors,

glad of my hands on the wheel
and the cloud of grit as it rises
where JCBs move motherly
widening the packed motorway.

Off-script

No, not a demonstration,
but each of us refusing

to learn our part.
The chorus dissolves
in ragged voices.

There is nothing for the director to work with.
We are quietly talking
off-script to one another –
'Yes, rhubarb with ginger –'

'Indeed we are all made from the dust of stars'

They are building houses
on rainwet fields
where the smoke of horses
has barely cleared –

indeed we are all made from the dust of stars,
even these houses are made from the dust of stars
whose light gallops towards us –

in the remotest corner
of the black-wet universe
there is a galaxy
of bright horses –

Tulip

How cool the lovely bulb of your roundness.
Bare-faced and sleek, you rise from your leaves.

You have the skin of a raindrop.
Blink, and your green flushes scarlet.

Poised on the catwalk of spring, you'll move
in your own time, smile when you want to.

Nothing comes up to you. Forget-me-nots
crowd at your roots, my fingers

hover, narcissi rustle
but you are still. Only the sun touches you.

Finger by finger it opens your petals
loosens the lovely bulb of your roundness,

makes you swagger in your exposure,
knows, as you don't, that it can't last long.

Beautiful today the

banana plants, camellia, echium, wild garlic flower's
rank tang of a more northern spring,
beautiful today the surf on Porthkidney Beach
and the standing out of the lighthouse, sheer
because of the rain past, the rain to come, the rain
that has brought this cliff-side to jungle thickness.

The hammock's green with a winter of rain, beautiful today
the bamboo, wrist-thick. Was it on this
foothold, this shelf, this terrace, it learned
to surf on a hiss of breeze, was it today
that taught this dry handshake of leaves
against the pull of tide on Porthkidney Beach?

A step, a seat, a stare to the east
where light springs from a wasteland
beyond where the wet sun dawns –
beautiful today, sun shakes from its shoulders
the night tides. In a wasteland of easterly light
sun makes play on the waves

but the hollow surf turns over and over
and nobody comes, only a track of footprints
runs to the sea, and the tall pines
make shapes of their limbs – beautiful today
the dazzle they capture as landscape,
the resin they ooze from their wounds.

White planks are full of washed-away footsteps, beautiful
today the graining of sweat and flesh. This shell
wears at its heart a coil
to last when the curves are gone – but today
the flush of light, the flowering of freckles
on tender skin are helplessly present

in the hour between pallor and sunburn,
while the banana plant wears its heart in a fist
of tiny fruit that will never ripen or open.
In the distance, the little town
waits for its saint to sail in on a leaf
for the second time, and bless its legion of roofs.

Dead gull on Porthmeor

You could use his wing as a fan
to rid yourself of dreams,

you could light a candle at midnight
in the flooded beach hut

and hear the wooden flute
waver its music

like a drop of rain
into a storm,

and the sea would prowl
along the black-wet horizon

and the sand would shine
as white as corn

ready for winnowing.
Yes, you could use his wing as a fan.

Narcissi

Everything changes to black and white –
the shaggy wreck of the Alba,
the shine of the neap tide

where the drowned funnels gulp for air
and the waves break like narcissi,

or the dog that skids to a stop, then quivers
all over, shaking a floss of water
to hide the Island.

The sea begins to smell of flowers
as the tide turns from its lair,

the narcissi flake off one by one
from that rust-bucket slumped in the sand –
the Alba's an old hand at drowning.

I was two when they first plumped me down
between Man's Head and the Island
where fox-trails of water ran out
over Porthmeor strand.

I smell something which reminds me
of not being born,
my mother walks on the shoreline

a figure or maybe a figurehead
with a smile of wood.

In the big glare of the white day
I clutch at the sand's
talkative hiss of grains,

lose my balance, and suddenly
scud on all fours
into the narcissi.

Dolphins whistling

Yes, we believed that the oceans were endless
surging with whales, serpents and mermaids,
demon-haunted and full of sweet voices
to lure us over the edge of the world,

we were conquerors, pirates, explorers, vagabonds
war-makers, sea-rovers, we ploughed
the wave's furrow, made maps
that led others to the sea's harvest

and sometimes we believed we heard dolphins whistling,
through the wine-dark waters we heard dolphins whistling.

We were restless and the oceans were endless,
rich in cod and silver-scaled herring
so thick with pilchard we dipped in our buckets
and threw the waste on the fields to rot,

we were mariners, fishers of Iceland, Newfoundlanders
fortune-makers, sea-rovers, we ploughed
the wave's furrow and earned our harvest
hungrily trawling the broad waters,

and sometimes we believed we heard dolphins whistling,
through blue-green depths we heard dolphins whistling.

The catch was good and the oceans were endless
so we fed them with run-off and chemical rivers
pair-fished them, scoured the sea-bed for pearls
and searched the deep where the sperm-whale plays,

we were ambergris merchants, fish farmers, cod-bank strippers
coral-crushers, reef-poisoners, we ploughed
the sea's furrow and seized our harvest
although we had to go far to find it

for the fish grew small and the whales were strangers,
coral was grey and cod-banks empty,
algae bloomed and the pilchards vanished
while the huer's lookout was sold for a chalet,

and the dolphins called their names to one another
through the dark spaces of the water
as mothers call their children at nightfall
and grow fearful for an answer.

We were conquerors, pirates, explorers, vagabonds
war-makers, sea-rovers, we ploughed
the wave's furrow, drew maps
to leads others to the sea's harvest,

and we believed that the oceans were endless
and we believed we could hear the dolphins whistling.

Borrowed light

Such a connoisseur of borrowed light!
Pale as a figurehead, undismayed
by the rough footpath
you climbed towards the view.

At the top, silent, you would breathe in
the spread of land you didn't care to own,
your face for a moment stern
and rapt, careless of children.

Such a connoisseur of borrowed light!
Even when your voice grew harsh
as those small stones rattling
down the adder path,

or when a January wind
harried cloud shadows
over the built-up valleys
you would climb as far as that boulder

where the view began,
and watch its unravelling.
You met equally
the landscape knitting itself

from russet, indigo
and crawling tractors,
or the blinding stare of the sea.

A winter imagination

Surely it's not too much to ask
from a winter imagination:

the clattering of chairs onto a pavement
the promptness of waiters before days waste them

and of course, the flickering of leaves,
the insouciant, constant

rapture of following the breeze.
Last night my daughter dreamed

that we would die, mother and father
gone while she stood watching.

I soothed her in my arms, promised her husband,
babies, troops of friends:

like the defences of a vulnerable kingdom
I named them, one by one. She slept rosily

but for me the bone-cold passages
still rang to her cry

You'll die and I'll be alone.

Surely it's not too much to ask
for a warm day to take away such dreams

for violet, midge-haunted shadows
under the sycamore that grows like a weed,

for this year's beautiful girls
to flaunt their bellies, while the boys

who won't stop talking, trot to keep up.
One of them is after my daughter

but her lovely eyes are blue with distance.
She is off at the gallop, dreamless.

Athletes

And what a load of leaf
there was on the trees by June.
From sticky fists
rammed in the eye of the bud
they'd opened wide,
and when the wind blew
the horse chestnuts were athletes
running with torches of green
in the half-marathon of summer.

Pneumonia

on our raft
after the long night of storm

the water bubbles
the sea is calm

the planks squeak lazily
where the ropes chafe them

the sea bulges
ready to open

why it should smell like jonquils
no one knows

the idling of the sun
changes everything

on our raft
after the long night of storm

the water bubbles
eye-level
why not watch it for ever

Wall is the book

(for Anne Stevenson)

Wall is the book of these old lands
each page scripted by stones,
each lichen frond, orange or golden,
wall's stubborn illumination.

Read wall slowly, for it takes time
to grasp the sentence of stone.
Wall breaks in a tumbled caesura
of boulders. Read on

where pucker of breeze on a tarn's shield
breaks the mirror of wall
and bog cotton trembles. It rains
on a draggle of sheep in the field

where wall breaks the force
and bite of steel from the north
whence weather and danger come.
Wall is the holy book of these old lands
each age scripted by stone.

Gorse

All through sour soil the gorse thrusts.
It is rough furze first, chopped to free the fields.
Burned off in sheets of carbon, it lives
down at the roots, grappling peat sponge,
black as an eclipse of the sun.

But when the gorse is out of blossom
kissing is then out of fashion.
Like ill-fitting shoes, gorse flowers
pinch and pinch until the sun touches them.

Now in the lanes a spice of coconut,
now the gorse thriving to wipe
the eye of winter with a cloth of gold,
now the bees in their bee kitchen

pilot themselves above the spines,
burrow past rapiers
bumbling, lunge into flowers
like drunks strangely kept safe
in a world full of harms,

and now it comes –
a prickle of intricate buds
a breath of perfume,
a flare along the roadways, a torch
barely mastered in the runner's arms
leaping the verges to set April alight.

Blackberries after Michaelmas

These blackberries belong to the devil.
Don't try to eat them now
or drop them in your pail.
Their flaccid sweetness

belongs to the one who ruined Adam,
set him to work in these hard fields
set him wallowing in green water
for pilchard and mackerel.

These blackberries are the devil's
and have his spit on them –
look where it settles.

To my nine-year-old self

You must forgive me. Don't look so surprised,
perplexed, and eager to be gone,
balancing on your hands or on the tightrope.
You would rather run than walk, rather climb than run
rather leap from a height than anything.

I have spoiled this body we once shared.
Look at the scars, and watch the way I move,
careful of a bad back or a bruised foot.
Do you remember how, three minutes after waking
we'd jump straight out of the ground floor window
into the summer morning?

That dream we had, no doubt it's as fresh in your mind
as the white paper to write it on.
We made a start, but something else came up –
a baby vole, or a bag of sherbet lemons –
and besides, that summer of ambition
created an ice-lolly factory, a wasp trap
and a den by the cesspit.

I'd like to say that we could be friends
but the truth is we have nothing in common
beyond a few shared years. I won't keep you then.
Time to pick rosehips for tuppence a pound,
time to hide down scared lanes
from men in cars after girl-children.

or to lunge out over the water
on a rope that swings from that tree
long buried in housing –
but no, I shan't cloud your morning. God knows
I have fears enough for us both –

I leave you in an ecstasy of concentration
slowly peeling a ripe scab from your knee
to taste it on your tongue.

Fallen angel

Waist-deep in snow and wading
through the world's cold,
this fallen angel with wings furled

on his way home from Bethlehem,
the story all told.
Centuries after the birth

through drab years with the promise fading
like gilt off the gold,
fallen angel still tramping the earth –

so long, the way back to Bethlehem
through the world's cold.

Bridal

Bride in the mud of the yard,
bare feet skilled to find
the nub of hard ground.

She stands as if she were transparent,
ears spiked, fingers encircled,
skirts stitched with metal.

Mud squelches through the keyhole
between first and second toe,
she slips, rescues herself.

Silence of banknotes
from sweaty hands, pinned to her dress
so the president's face shows.

She drives the cows in
through velvet of shit and slime,
their soiled tails switching

their dirty udders craving release
as women crave the gums of their babies
in the first shudder of feeding.

In the silence of the marriage night
with a befuddled bridegroom
too old for the task at hand
she will not cry out.

Bride in the mud of the yard,
thirteen and hopping
through velvet of cowshit
from stone to stone.

Still life with ironing

I love it when you look at me like this,
and the washed smell of your blue denim
We are washed out, the two of us,
shadows of what we have been.

A moth in the bowl of a paper lampshade,
a gust of night and a baby's cry,
a drop of milk on the wrist, inside
where the blood beats time.

Sometimes a heatwave is too much to take.
We are not up to it, up for it,
bare enough, blank enough. We fake
pleasure but turn towards evening,

to the clink of a glass, the settling of blackbirds
the talkative hose in the next garden,
a shirt with the buttons undone
and shadows put in by the iron.

Spanish Irish

It is your impulse I remember,
the movement that made you your own,
the way you laughed when you were told
some daily but delightful thing,
and the way you could not be fooled.

When I saw that man who recalled you
I put out my hand to keep him
as if his Spanish Irish face
must lighten in recognition,
and I was on the point of speaking
the pleasure of your name.

Cowboys

They rode the ridge those five minutes
I was caught in traffic
watching nothing but rain
falling on slate,

they rode the beauty of angles,
they laddered oblivion
and saved their own lives eight times
as their boots spun,

they rode without harness
astride the ridge of the roof,
they chucked a rope around the chimney
before it galloped off,

they rode in a rain-sweat,
they might have fallen like snow,
they hollered across the prairie
until the roofs echoed.

Below Hungerford Bridge

Below Hungerford Bridge the river
oils its own surface like a seabird.
Tide fights with current, crowds
surge to a concert, the light thickens.

How unaccountable the dead are:
I think you rear from your photograph
with an expression of terror: *I can't move.*
Will you let me out of here?

I think I see T.S. Eliot
wan in his green make-up
but slyly playful, a big cat
gone shabby with keeping.

The traffic halts. There's nothing
but a few pile-driven wharves
and the river remembering
its old courses.

Ophelia

I dreamed my love became a boat
on the saltings in winter
after long treading the green water,

I dreamed my love flew to the bar
where the tide teemed with the river,
and bucked and fought there,

I dreamed that my love's timber
was a bed for eelgrass
and marsh samphire,

I dreamed my love became a boat
on the saltings in winter
after long treading the green water,

and beneath his shroud of skin
was a rib chamber
for winds to whistle in.

Winter bonfire

My mind aches where I cannot touch it.
It has put a net over some words,
it is hiding a poem.

Who is that man tending flames in his garden,
and why does he heap armfuls of paper
on his winter bonfire?

If I write down anything
no matter how stealthily
the poem will know it.

One A.M.

Melancholy at one A.M. –
the poem ended
or else just quietly
lying under the table
gnawing the bone of its being –

the lighthouse in its bowl of sea
the town by its holy well
and the owls hunting.

Surf hollows the base of the cliffs,
owls hollow the safety of night
and the poem makes its rest
by turning and turning
like a hare in its form.

Lemon and stars

The stars come so close
they seem not to be shining
but to be remaking the world
in their own pattern

and we seem to be caught in their dust
like the fingerprints of creatures
not yet imagined.
Besides, there is the starlight

not enough to make star-shadow
but enough, in the absence of moon
to heap up darkness
just here, under the lemon tree.

Cutting open the lemons

After all they didn't taste of salt
or the winter storms.

I had not expected the insides to be so
offhandedly daffodil –

lemons should be more malleable
to the imagination –

but like babies they are sure
that the planting and tending

gives no right over them.

Hearing owls

The dark fabric of night not torn
but seamed with the flight of owls
hunting the margin of the Downs.

The houses pull their roofs over them,
the sleepers plunge beneath their bedclothes
at the onrush of wings,

the mouse runs with its trail of urine.
The owl pulls off a miracle
as it homes in

like a jump-jet in mid-Atlantic
sighting its landing area
in a waste of sea slop.

The mouse is done. The owl swallows
while a car passes, knowing nothing
of the owl agape at its own fortune.

'Often they go just before dawn'

A wash of stars covers the sky
before the day comes,
before the slippery quickness of brush-strokes
dries to a surface,

a wash of stars covers the sky
announcing with pallor
that they are going out
or that something else –

call it a day, or dawn –
is about to come in.
Quick, quick, get up the ladder
and paint in more brightness

for the stars to be dark against.

May voyage

A May evening and a bright moon
riding easily in its mystery,
you come out onto the balcony
and gaze there, relaxed, intent
as the horizon softens towards France
and the moon voyages, voyages.

What storms have you seen!
Such a hurricane
when wind hurled around the building
like an express train,
but you fought it out of your home
and now you note the turning of the tide
as the moon voyages, voyages

from peace into deeper peace
from old age into youth,
behind you the French windows are open
ahead of you only the shining
sea and the lovely work of the moon
as it voyages, voyages
into the calm.